The SAS Story

SAS re-enactor in typical Gulf War-type garb stands before a replica Pink Panther desert vehicle. These heavily armed Land Rovers are reminiscent of the jeeps and trucks used by their forefathers in the SAS and Long Range Desert Group during the Second World War. (John Blackman)

The SAS Story

Mike Morgan

Sutton Publishing

SAS re-enactor mimics the classic action pose captured in a famous Second World War photograph of L Detachment SAS in the desert. (John Blackman)

First published in the United Kingdom in 2008 by
Sutton Publishing, an imprint of The History Press
Cirencester Road · Chalford · Stroud · Gloucestershire · GL6 8PE

British Library Cataloguing in Publication Data
A catalogue record for this book is available from the British
Library.

Hardback ISBN 978-0-7509-4840-1

Typeset in 9.5/14.5pt Syntax.
Typesetting and origination by
The History Press.
Printed and bound in the United Kingdom.

CONTENTS

This book has been written as a concise, informative and accurate guide to the SAS Regiment, the most famous Special Force in the world.

It is principally aimed at all those who are interested in the SAS, but who want to know more about the Regiment without wading through hefty historical volumes of regimental history. It is also aimed at younger readers who require a comprehensive and stimulating photographic display, allied to a clear and easily assimilated text, full of key facts and figures. It in no way pretends to be a full historical record of the SAS – this has been done many times elsewhere. However, studying these pages will give any reader an excellent idea of the history of the SAS and the training, tactics and capabilities of its soldiers and officers – hand-picked from the cream of the British Army.

➤
Formation of replica jeeps and SAS desert raiders. (John Blackman)

Snapshot comments and eyewitness personal memories by retired SAS veterans make the text burst into life in what truly is a unique and exciting new format.

Mike Morgan is author of *Daggers Drawn*, *Real Heroes of the SAS and SBS*, *Sting of the Scorpion*, *D-Day Hero* and *Geordie – Fighting Legend of the Modern SAS* for Sutton Publishing.

Ex-11th Scottish Commando and L Detachment, 1st SAS and SRS veteran L/Cpl Denis Bell (rear left) and comrades 'behind the lines' in France,1944. (Denis Bell/Mike Morgan)

ACKNOWLEDGEMENTS

First, I would like to thank two former SAS veterans and personal friends who have given invaluable help and guidance, ensuring that the factual veracity of this book is as accurate as possible: Graham 'Tommo' Thomson and Geordie Doran, formerly of 22 SAS and co-author with me of *Geordie – Fighting Legend of the Modern SAS* (Sutton Publishing). They have both served with distinction at the sharp end of conflicts and know the Regiment and its soldiers as well as anyone.

I also pay tribute to stirring memories recalled from late, great SAS veterans of the Second World War: Denis Bell, L Detachment, 1st SAS and SRS comrade of Lt Col Paddy Mayne DSO and three bars, Bill Hackney, 1st SAS and SBS comrade of Maj Anders Lassen VC, MC and two bars, and Arthur Arger, original member of Y Patrol, Long Range Desert Group (LRDG) and comrade of the unit's Commander Lt Col David Lloyd Owen DSO, MC.

Photographer John Blackman has provided some brilliant re-enactment photographs of SAS and LRDG personnel, equipment and vehicles.

I also thank my good friend Gary Hull from Belfast for his kind help in providing information and photographs, my daughter Jenny for some superb close-up photographs and my wife Penny for her skill with computers. Thanks also to the late George Daniels MM, SAS veteran Arthur Huntbach and my pal Steve James.

The biggest tribute is to David Stirling's brilliant and totally original SAS concept – and the courageous men who continue to make it work in a challenging and ever-changing world.

The SAS – the British Special Air Service – is so famous, feared, admired and envied worldwide in the cloak-and-dagger field of Special Forces that it seems to have been around forever.

In fact, it has been in existence merely in excess of six decades, during which time the force has taken part in some of the most ground-breaking events in history and established an immense reputation which has yet to be equalled.

Its tough, specially selected troops and officers have been forged and honed in the white-hot conflict of danger-packed operations behind the lines in the Second World War, Malaya, Oman, the Falklands, Sierra Leone, Afghanistan, Iraq, two Gulf Wars and numerous other trouble spots, to create a regiment which is today second to none in experience, training and capability.

Some people confuse the role of the SAS with that of out-and-out combat troops. Britain certainly has some of the finest fighting soldiers in the world in the form of the Paras, the Commandos, the Guards, the Gurkhas and countless other regiments. It is also a fact that many worthy VCs and top awards have been won time and again in the course of history from the most unlikely of units and individuals, illustrating that bravery has no boundaries.

Although the SAS is often called upon to fight in action as hard as, if not harder than, its Regular Army comrades in behind-the-lines fire fights, ambushes and special operations, this is not its only role. Often the SAS soldier can be engaged in unglamorous, but vital tasks, such as being up to his waist in water camouflaged by vegetation on covert surveillance of an

Inspection by the Duke of Gloucester of SAS stripping Spandau machine guns and Schmeissers in the Western Desert. (IWM E12971)

SAS jeep, heavily armed with Browning and Vickers K machine guns. (IWM NA676)

enemy position, lying motionless for hours or days at a time to get a sniping shot at a key target, or using urban 'hides' to track the movements of terrorists or enemy forces to report vital information to higher command.

To support their special 'behind enemy lines' role, SAS soldiers have always had a choice of the best weapons available. In the Second World War this meant troops used a mixture of Vickers K machine guns, Thompson sub-machine guns, American Colt 45 and Browning pistols and M1 carbines and Tommy guns. They used captured German Schmeisser sub-machine guns, which were considered far superior to their Allied counterparts. In more recent times they have used American M16 rifles, sometimes with grenade launchers, Heckler and Koch sub-machine guns, Armalite rifles, Minimi light machine guns and many others, including the finest hand guns available.

The overall role of the SAS is currently extremely complex and varied – much more so than there is scope for in this concise introduction. However, versatility has always been one of the Regiment's strong points – and its soldiers have always risen to respond with great courage and skill to any task asked of them. Many of these operations have not only required patience and ultra-cautious surveillance skills and using laser-guided bomb targeting for warplanes attacking enemy targets, they have also involved full-blooded action using SAS soldiers on the ground in attack mode, employing the key advantages of surprise, training and split second co-ordination. Prime examples include the

audacious destruction of some of Saddam Hussein's mobile Scud missile launchers by SAS infiltrators using Pink Panther jeeps and foot-slogging across the desert in the Gulf War against Iraq in 1991, just like their Second World War forebears.

This versatility was never emphasised more superbly than in the Iranian Embassy Siege crisis in London in 1980 when – using secret and well-practised techniques and methods – daring teams of SAS stormed the building and rescued most of the hostages in the full glare of the world's media, as a later chapter describes more fully. Today the SAS still leads the field in hostage-busting situations.

The men of the SAS can genuinely be described as special themselves, but indisputably, the man the world has to thank for the formation of the SAS is

Lieutenant, later Lieutenant Colonel and ultimately Sir David Stirling, who operated with breathtaking élan with the original unit – L Detachment SAS – in the Western Desert in 1941. Stirling's fledgling Special Force formation hammered the exposed flank of Field Marshal Rommel's troops, convoys and especially his aerodromes, which were strung temptingly across the desert. The plans to creep up and plant bombs directly on enemy aircraft were amazingly bold. Many in High Command thought his ideas foolhardy, if not insane, but Stirling was vindicated when his raiders destroyed hundreds of Hitler's best fighters and bombers on the ground.

Stirling was the linchpin behind the initial 'private army' scheme of the SAS and he had several distinct advantages in his armoury. He was incredibly brave, a legendary planner and gifted Special Forces thinker, the like of which the British Army would not see again during the Second World War, and he had friends in the highest of places, including the British Military High Command. He also had the ear of top politicians, including Winston Churchill. Consequently, he, unlike others, had the ability to make things happen.

But Stirling's untimely capture by the Germans in 1943, while trying to link up with American forces in Tunisia, was one of the worst disasters ever for the SAS. Imprisoned in the near escape-proof Colditz Castle for the rest of the war, the SAS lost its vital guiding hand, though others – notably the legendary Lt Col Paddy Mayne DSO and three bars – heroically led the SAS to further glory.

Fortunately Stirling survived to influence the workings of the postwar SAS and had

a key and sometimes covert hand in world affairs for decades to come.

During the Second World War, two British SAS units, 1st and 2nd SAS, operated in various theatres of war, alongside two French regiments and one Belgian.

The author's late father, Cpl Jack Morgan, who had served earlier in the Eighth Army's desert battles in the RASC, was an original veteran of the 2nd Special Air Service Regiment from its foundation at Philippeville, North Africa, in 1943. He became a member of the elite SAS Intelligence Section under Maj Eric Barkworth for the remainder of the war, operating in North Africa and Italy and planning for the SAS drops in Europe after D-Day and the occupation of Norway in 1945.

Through this connection, the author has been privileged to meet many SAS

Cpl Jack Morgan of the 2nd SAS Intelligence unit, Italy, 1944. (Morgan collection)

The author with Paddy Mayne's service revolver holster from Mayne's time with the Royal Ulster Rifles, before joining the SAS. (Author's Collection)

veterans of all conflicts at reunions at the SAS Credenhill HQ near Hereford and elsewhere, on numerous occasions. All the SAS soldiers whom the author has met have been exceptional characters, possessing the ability to do extraordinary things, yet dignified and modest despite their considerable achievements.

The extra indefinable something which sets the men of the SAS apart will become clearer in the following pages. But, as one seasoned SAS veteran once quipped to the author by way of explanation: 'If it were possible to break an SAS soldier in half, like a stick of rock, he would almost invariably have *Who Dares Wins* written boldly right through his body!'

Who dares contradict that?

Many people think the typical SAS recruit is built like Rambo – 6ft 3in of rippling muscle, with bulging biceps and a gung-ho attitude to put John Wayne and the American Marines to shame.

In reality, nothing could be further from the truth. Admittedly there are some tall and powerfully built he-men among the ranks of Britain's Special Forces and these individuals undoubtedly fit the stereotype image of the SAS, but the majority are of average build, of deceptively average disposition, modest, sometimes quietly spoken – the sort who would blend into a crowd with ease, as they often have to on active duty, sometimes employing various foreign or civilian disguises.

The recruits are invariably intelligent, tough, supremely fit, well-trained, totally self-reliant, brave and determined. The one

Replica LRDG Chevrolet truck and crew manning heavy weapons, crests a sand dune. (John Blackman)

Did you know?

During the Second World War, the SAS destroyed more than 400 of the Germans' best warplanes on the ground in North Africa. This had a crucial bearing on the final victory in the Western Desert.

An original 1941 Egypt SAS cap badge made by an Arab tailor. (Private collection/Laura Morgan)

quality which all SAS men need to keep one step ahead of the opposition is the ability never to give up, to keep going in the most testing of circumstances, to overcome every challenge no matter how hard and no matter how physically or mentally difficult. A good sense of humour is also a godsend, allied with utter faith in one's own abilities and those of the comrades who, in turn, rely on you.

One of the most experienced and widely served former veterans of 22 SAS, Warrant Officer Class II Geordie Doran, voiced similar forthright opinions of his fellow SAS troopers and officers in a recent interview with the author. Geordie served with distinction in the Paras and later saw much action in the SAS in Malaya, Borneo, Oman and Yemen.

He said: 'The popular public image of an SAS soldier is usually that of a tall, good-looking James Bond type, with a broad-shouldered, muscular torso and steely eyes looking out from a ruggedly handsome face. *Nothing* could be further from the truth.

'In my experience this type was very few and far between. During my long service in the SAS I saw all sorts of characters – there were short, medium, skinny, broad, tall and gangling types, with every colour of skin

'The SAS wants someone who is brave, fit, determined and intelligent. Above all, a soldier who will never give up.'

Retired SAS Warrant Officer II Geordie Doran, veteran of 22 SAS and former Permanent Staff Instructor for 23 TA SAS.

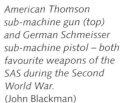

American Thomson sub-machine gun (top) and German Schmeisser sub-machine pistol – both favourite weapons of the SAS during the Second World War.
(John Blackman)

Original Egypt wings of a brave L Detachment SAS veteran of the Western Desert, and a 1944 SAS cloth cap badge. These rare wings were worn in action in all the famous 1st SAS actions in the Desert, Sicily, Italy, France and Germany, including the operation in Germany in 1945 in which Lt Col Paddy Mayne was recommended for – but never received – the Victoria Cross. (Private collection/Jenny Morgan)

'The Regiment requires the right raw material to turn a keen volunteer into the best there is.'

Retired SAS WOII Geordie Doran.

and hair, and not many of them were handsome. In fact, there was not – and by what I have seen *is* not – a set type of SAS man.

'There is also a grand mix of places where soldiers come from who join the Regiment. You will find men from every unit in the British Army and many are from the Parachute Regiment and Royal Marines.

'There is no part of the UK predominantly represented in SAS ranks either. A quick stocktake today would find Jocks, Welsh, Irish, Geordies, Scousers, Cockneys, Swedes (our name for those from the South-west), in fact blokes from every county in Britain.

Also, during and after World War Two there were men from many Commonwealth countries; plus the Australians and New Zealanders had, and still have, their own SAS. The Rhodesian SAS was originally part of 22 SAS (C Squadron) in the Malayan campaign against communist guerrillas in the 1950s. On return to Rhodesia they took part in the independence struggle, but were disbanded afterwards when Rhodesia became independent of Britain and was renamed Zimbabwe.

'There has also never been any racism exhibited in the unit. In the SAS, if a man passed Selection and was a good soldier then he was accepted regardless of colour, religion or nationality – or even how ugly he was! Some of the finest recruits have come from Fiji and elsewhere.

'But what I think is an outstanding attribute for SAS men is a rugged sense of humour without which life, in or out of action, can be very miserable. Taking the mickey out of each other is a daily routine and another essential quality in the Regiment is comradeship. There is genuine concern for one another, whether in or out of action.

'Watching each other's backs, in any situation, was always normal procedure. There were a few exceptions – sometimes you would pinch your mate's girlfriend, OK, but never his rations or ammunition!'

In short, what makes a soldier a good SAS man is essentially the same today as it would have been when the unit was first formed by David Stirling in the Second World War.

Did you know?

Soldiers only get two chances at passing Selection for the SAS. After that no more attempts are allowed.

The selection process for the SAS is arguably the toughest training regime for any armed force anywhere in the world, including all rival Special Forces.

The current process was officially introduced in 1952/3 by Lt Col John Woodhouse, Commanding Officer of 22 SAS Regiment, and the Selection course, which has changed remarkably little over the years, traditionally focuses on the rain and windswept Brecon Beacons in Wales. This bleak and unforgiving terrain comprises a series of towering peaks and thickly grassed, energy-sapping steep slopes – an area notorious for its inhospitable weather and unpredictable, sudden and potentially dangerous changes in climate. Courses take place in summer and winter irrespective of weather conditions.

Candidates are well aware that taking part in the SAS Selection process can be a lethal experience, in which they are driven close to the limits of human endurance. A number of participants have died, including one soldier who sat down briefly to rest on the top of Pen y Fan mountain, having successfully conquered most of the course, only to lose consciousness and succumb to hypothermia caused by the biting wind, rain and cold.

Such fatalities led to more stringent safety measures which have reduced the risk, but, nevertheless, it is recognised by Special Forces chiefs the world over that the inherent dangers of such tough training regimes and processes can never be eliminated completely and this remains the case to the present day.

In the earliest days of the formation of the SAS Regiment, a pioneering form of the Selection process was operated from

The formidable, compact and heavily armed SAS jeep is shown to perfection in this re-enactment shot. (John Blackman)

1941 by Lt Jock Lewes in the Western Desert. Lewes was one of the key officers who helped form the fledgling SAS under David Stirling.

In addition to physical training, navigation and practise on rudimentary parachute training apparatus, weaker soldiers were weeded out at an early stage by various endurance tests and marches and those who failed were smartly RTU'd (returned to their unit), never to appear among the ranks of the SAS again. The training in the desert included long marches with little food and water carried. Lewes often cunningly judged distances travelled by carrying a pocket full of small pebbles, transferring a stone from one pocket to the other every few hundred yards, so that he could later obtain an accurate 'fix' on his position by counting up the pebbles transferred and by using his compass and his own calculations. These marches encouraged incredible feats of endurance and stamina. On one occasion Trooper John Sillito MM, when separated from his comrades after a fierce fire fight on a raid near Tobruk in 1942, walked more than 180 miles to reach British forces across burning desert with virtually nothing to drink or eat. This superhuman effort earned him a well-deserved Military Medal and could not have been achieved without the tough early training of the SAS which developed huge reserves of fitness, willpower and stamina.

Nearly fifty years later, in the First Gulf War, SAS veteran Chris Ryan was the only member of an eight-man team to escape from Iraq. He was part of the Bravo Two Zero squad, of which three

➤
Trooper John Sillito MM, one of an SAS unit despatched to blow up the railway line near Alamein. (IWM E19781)

➤➤
Bill Hackney, wartime veteran of the 1st SAS and comrade of SBS Maj Anders Lassen VC, MC and two bars. (Courtesy of the author)

'Whatever you do, don't stop. Just keep putting one foot in front of the other. If you sit down to take five, you could freeze to death.'

SAS instructor to Geordie Doran when he completed his Selection course on the Brecon Beacons in the winter of 1957/8.

colleagues died and four were captured. Covering around 200 miles on foot in just seven days, in searing daytime heat and freezing temperatures at night, it was the longest escape in the history of the SAS and for this Ryan was also awarded the Military Medal. He successfully reached Syria, which had previously agreed to return any escaped Coalition service personnel.

Bill Hackney, from Middlesbrough, a late good friend of the author and a seasoned veteran of 1st SAS and later Special Boat Squadron comrade of the legendary

Danish Maj Anders Lassen VC, MC and two bars, told the author a revealing story about his own introduction to the Selection process in 1942. Bill said: 'I was coming to the end of this 25-mile march at the jog, carrying a 70lb pack on my back. I thought I had done pretty well and kept up a good pace when, approaching the finishing line, one of the SAS instructors ran up alongside me and berated me for my lack of fitness, calling me a disgrace to my unit and a lot of other unprintable names. Finally he barked the order: "Go round again"!'

Desperately fatigued and swaying and sweating under his heavy load, Bill staggered over the finishing line and reluctantly started on his way to another 25 miles of torture. After 250yds he collapsed in a heap, overcome with exhaustion, and though he tried manfully to rise again, he could not

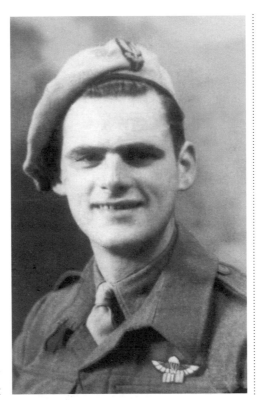

Did you know?
When SAS soldiers qualify as parachutists they are awarded a set of wings to wear on their uniforms. These were originally designed in Egypt and the wings are said to be modelled on the feathers of the Ibis bird, bisected by a parachute symbol in the centre.

SAS Fairbairn Sykes dagger and sheath from a Malaya campaign veteran. (Private collection/Katie Morgan)

Second World War LRDG scorpion cap badge. (Private collection/Jenny Morgan)

get to his feet to continue. The same SAS instructor ran up to him and said in a cheery voice: 'You've passed, you'll do for us!'

Bill explained that the instructors were just trying to see if he would go that little bit extra under pressure, without giving up. Afterwards, he realised if he

◄

Replica of the famous 'Blitz Buggy' as used by David Stirling and SAS comrades in early behind-the-lines raids in the Western Desert – successfully deceiving the Germans into believing it was one of their own staff cars.
(John Blackman)

had stopped before the finish line, he would have failed, but because he was prepared to go on, even only for a few more yards, he exhibited that stubborn quality so vital to SAS requirements.

SAS SELECTION TODAY

Selection is open to all regiments of the British Army and the TA (21 and 23) Regiments of the SAS. Paras and Commando candidates tend to do well, as these units have their own extremely tough training and fitness regimes in place. The British SAS also trains members from the Commonwealth and the Republic of Ireland. In fact, the Regiment has always had a strong representation from Northern and Southern Ireland, as well as Wales and Scotland.

Modern SAS Selection focuses on endurance, strength, high-level fitness and determination. Nowadays the course covers a six-month test, utilising the Brecon Beacons and the Elan Valley in Wales and a jungle course in Asia, usually Brunei. Live ammunition is often used in exercises.

Selection is held biannually, summer and winter, regardless of conditions. Candidates must be male Regular members of the Armed Forces who have served for at least three years. However, TA members of 21 SAS or 23 SAS can apply after serving for eighteen months. All soldiers must be under 32 years of age and have at least thirty-nine months of military service left to complete.

Any candidates failing any of the stages of Selection are RTU'd, i.e. returned to their parent unit. The maximum number of attempts at Selection allowed is two.

2nd SAS shoulder title, as worn by the author's late father, Cpl Jack Morgan in the Second World War, and a wartime SAS cap badge. (Jenny Morgan)

KEY PHASES OF SELECTION

Endurance Candidates have to complete a long-distance 40-mile hike on the Brecon Beacons, plus a shorter timed run of around 8 miles within an hour. On the long-distance test, candidates must carry a rifle

The replica SAS Blitz Buggy and armed SAS jeep in the background. (John Blackman)

Arthur Huntbach, 2nd SAS (right) and his comrades celebrating victory at Ostend with a captured Nazi flag, 1945. (Courtesy of Arthur Huntbach)

17

and pack weighing upwards of 70lb. Going up and down the notorious Pen y Fan mountain on the infamous 'Fan Dance' part of the course invariably requires running on the way down to give sufficient time for the numerous long, back-breaking climbs to the summit.

Mock combat This test is usually held in Asia, with soldiers using their wits and skills to give the 'enemy' forces the slip.

Escape and survival Candidates who have reached this stage are given a kit of limited items, such as fish hooks and snares, which they must use to catch fish, snakes or game to live off for several days while evading an 'enemy' force tracking them. Finally, soldiers must surrender at a set rendezvous. 'Enemy' captors then subject them to a tough mock interrogation which includes physical and mental abuse designed to cause maximum stress. All those who pass this final, harrowing test, win coveted entry into the SAS Regiment.

David Stirling will forever be remembered in the history of warfare as the brilliant and highly revered founding father of the Special Air Service. Without his rare genius, stupendous determination, high-flying connections and crystal clear vision of the type of unit required during the Second World War to attack and cripple the German forces, the SAS would never have got off the ground. It is also a salutary thought that if events had taken a slightly different course on several crucial occasions

◄
A column of SAS re-enactors set off on patrol in Western Desert conditions led by a Paddy Mayne lookalike officer. (John Blackman)

19

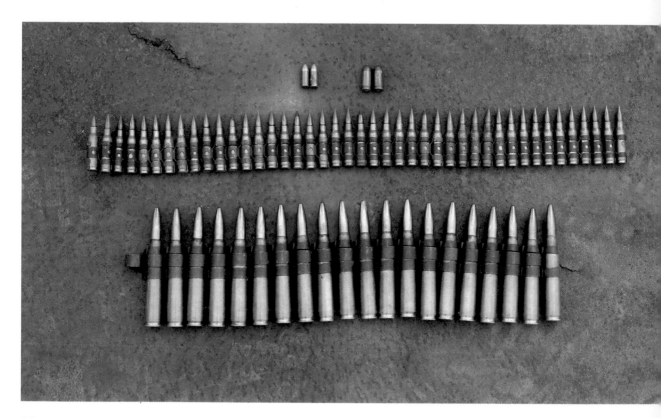

◄◄
Various calibres of ammunition for SAS weapons including (from the top, left to right): 9mm, .45, 7.62mm and .5. The smaller calibres are for pistols and sub-machine guns, the larger for rifles and light machine guns, and the largest for heavy calibre machine guns. (John Blackman)

◄
SAS re-enactment enthusiasts and armed jeeps line up for the camera in this shot which is typical of the desert days of the Second World War. (John Blackman)

both during and since the Second World War, Britain would not have the world famous SAS Special Force – and all its accumulated experience, skill and resources – to call on to fight in conflicts worldwide today.

When the unit was formed in the fiery crucible of the Western Desert in 1941, Britain was experiencing the first of a series of crushing defeats by that other military genius of the Second World War – Rommel. In a classic David and Goliath scenario, Stirling hatched a master plan to trounce German domination with minimum manpower, explosives and raw British courage. Within eighteen months, his fledgling SAS force would destroy a huge part of Hitler's vaunted desert air force and have a key effect on the ultimate Allied victory in the Desert War. To achieve this seemingly impossible goal he had the help of many brave and committed people – including fellow officers Jock Lewes, Paddy Mayne and other tough, uncompromising soldiers from various parent regiments.

Many years later, at the opening of the SAS base at Stirling Lines, near Hereford, Stirling chivalrously paid tribute to several of these fellow officers as 'co-founders' of the Regiment. But the massive void left by his capture at the hands of rival German Special Forces in Tunisia in 1943 was a blow to the SAS, which robbed the unit of its tactical mastermind for the remainder of the war. Stirling was the one man who could never be replaced.

The SAS was a development of the Commandos, a force enthusiastically backed by Britain's pugnacious war leader, Winston

Churchill. However, Stirling's brainwave was that small groups of teams of four raiders each slipping silently through enemy lines could wreak havoc, whereas large parties of seaborne attackers would be detected and destroyed.

At the time of the Desert War, a consignment of parachutes bound for the 2nd Parachute Brigade in India was waylaid by Lt Jock Lewes, of No. 8 Commando, based at Alexandria. Lewes, an adventurous officer and close friend of Stirling, obtained permission to experiment with the parachutes. Stirling joined the band of intrepid fellow Commandos, but jumping from an old Valencia bomber he badly damaged his spine and was temporarily paralysed. Undaunted, he put his convalescence in the Scottish Military Hospital in Alexandria to excellent use

LRDG scorpion plaque badge, made by craftsman Len Brown. This is one of a handful made to a long lost pattern found in LRDG Association archives by the author, which was never produced as an official plaque due to the high cost of manufacture. (Courtesy of the author/ Jenny Morgan)

and wrote his famous report arguing that current Commando raids were too large and that groups of around sixty men divided into four-man patrols should be parachuted

Lt Col Paddy Mayne wearing the famous beige beret prior to D-Day, 1944. (IWM AP6069)

into the desert instead. Using explosives, raiders could strike at enemy airfields on the vulnerable coastal plain, slipping in stealthily from the exposed desert flank. Afterwards, they would melt away into the darkness to rendezvous with the Long Range Desert Group, who would bring them back by truck to British lines.

The plan was daringly practical. So, after being discharged from hospital in July, Stirling wangled his way into the office of the Deputy Commander of the British Army, Gen Ritchie, using cheek and good luck to get top-level backing for his scheme. The plan also appealed to the Commander-in-Chief, Gen Auchinleck, who was working on a big new offensive and wanted Stirling's special operation to help guarantee its success. Manpower for Stirling's tiny force came from the Layforce

Replica Ford LRDG truck and jeep, similar to those used by the Desert SAS. (John Blackman)

group of Commando units, which was being disbanded and gave access to highly trained soldiers skilled in close-quarter fighting and demolition.

At the end of July 1941, the SAS was born. The grandiose choice of name, L Detachment Special Air Service Brigade, was suggested by Brig Dudley Clarke, one of the instigators of the Commandos. He was using many ruses at this time, including dummy planes and equipment, to deceive the Axis forces about the strength of British formations in North Africa. Clarke dubbed one of these bogus units 1st Special Air Service Brigade and asked Stirling to call his parachute unit L Detachment Special Air Service Brigade to fool the Germans into believing that much larger British forces existed.

◄
Sand dunes, jeeps, machine guns and SAS re-enactors recreate a scene played out many times in the Western Desert when Stirling's L Detachment was at its peak. (John Blackman)

By August, Stirling was authorised by Auchinleck to recruit 66 Commandos from Layforce and the fledgling SAS unit was established at Kabrit, a village in the Canal Zone about 100 miles from Cairo. There were just three months to complete training before the first mission by the SAS, timed to coincide with Auchinleck's November offensive.

Stirling's handpicked officers were Lewes, Mayne, Fraser, Thomas, Bonnington, and McGonigal. Mayne was an unpredictable firebrand who Stirling recruited despite the fact that he was under arrest for striking his former commanding officer. In the event, Mayne repaid Stirling's faith in him a thousand fold and he became one of the most famous commanding SAS officers of all time – and one of the most highly decorated soldiers of the war with four DSOs and numerous foreign honours.

Training in explosives, navigation and night movement forged ahead. The SAS also became expert in handling all Allied and Axis weapons. Some even preferred to carry in combat superior German weapons such as the Schmeisser machine pistol. From then on, the SAS had the choice of the best weapons available, whether American, British or German.

Improvised parachute training included, famously, Stirling and his men making backward rolls off 3-ton lorries racing across the desert at speeds up to 50mph. This caused many injuries. When parachute training jumps from an old RAF Bristol Bombay began, the first two troopers out of the aircraft plunged to their deaths because the static line clips on their chutes failed. The clips were strengthened to solve the problem and Stirling showed his courage by electing to jump first the next day, fearlessly leading by example.

Meanwhile, Jock Lewes spent many hours perfecting his famous 'sticky bomb' secret weapon – a combined explosive and incendiary charge of thermite and plastic explosive, designed to destroy aircraft on the ground. Nothing like this had ever existed before.

The deadline for Auchinleck's offensive arrived on 16 November 1941 and the SAS boarded aircraft to parachute in and slip undetected to attack a cluster of German frontline airfields housing some of the Luftwaffe's best fighters and bombers. However, the worst desert storms for years turned the mission into a disaster. Of more than sixty officers and men in five groups dropped from Bristol Bombay aircraft, only twenty-two returned from the raid. Strong winds scattered the SAS raiders across the desert. Some were killed or severely hurt on landing and others were lost on the ground. Some were captured, but not shot as ordered by Hitler, as the chivalrous Rommel refused to carry out such atrocities. None of the target airfields were attacked because all the weapons and bomb containers were lost in the mayhem. Miraculously, the key men, including Stirling and Mayne, lived to fight another day. As arranged, the LRDG picked up the survivors to take them back to Allied lines. Wily LRDG Commander, David Lloyd Owen, suggested to Stirling that in future instead of parachuting in, the SAS could be taken to their targets by the LRDG and then picked up on the way back. This simple idea saved the force from disbandment.

The LRDG, formed by Ralph Bagnold in June 1940, drove specially modified Chevrolet and Ford trucks bristling with heavy machine guns. They sometimes raided bases and airfields, but their main role was intelligence gathering, carrying British agents to and from their destinations, patrolling deeply behind enemy lines, operating clandestine road watches to count the strength of enemy convoys and, later, finding new routes through the desert for larger forces to outflank the enemy. Once the SAS had its own 'taxi service' to take it on its deadly missions, in the shape of the LRDG, the High Command gave Stirling's men a precious second chance.

Gen Ritchie, now C-in-C of the Eighth Army, ordered L Detachment to Jalo oasis, which it shared with a unit of the LRDG. Spectacular success soon followed in December 1941, with SAS squads simultaneously attacking enemy airfields at Sirte, Agheila and Agedabia, destroying more than sixty enemy aircraft and thirty vehicles with their Lewes bombs.

Stirling and Mayne hit airfields at Tamet and Sirte just before Christmas, while Lewes and his party attacked a similar target at Nofilia. Mayne's Irish luck held again at Tamet and, as well as bombs set on aircraft, there was an infamous incident when he burst into the pilots' mess on the airfield, causing a bloodbath with his

'Raids like this were the reason why SAS training had to be so hard . . . We didn't just blast our way in. Stealth, surprise and timing were crucial.'

L Detachment SAS veteran L/Cpl Denis Bell tells of the high emotions created by dangerous desert operations behind enemy lines.

Thompson sub-machine gun fitted with a 50-round drum magazine. For good measure Mayne ripped the instrument panel out of the last plane they came across with his bare hands, because he had run out of bombs. Lewes was killed on the way back from Nofilia when his column of vehicles was strafed by an enemy plane. As one of the unit's key strategists and its training supremo, his loss was keenly felt.

The raiders wore with pride their famous cap badge of a flaming sword of Excalibur over the legendary motto 'Who Dares Wins' on their sand-coloured berets. White berets were issued initially, but soon ditched as they provoked fights in Cairo bars with rival units. Stirling is thought to have coined the famous motto, but as the first badges were made by a local tailor, the flaming sword

became a winged dagger – and it stuck! The dark and light blue colours represented the Oxford and Cambridge University rowing backgrounds of the SAS officers involved. Highly prized parachute wings in white and two-tone blue were worn on the right upper arm of troopers after five jumps. Officers wore these on the left breast and, after a number of completed missions, other ranks did the same. The men prized these wings more than any medals.

The SAS went from strength to strength, destroying more enemy aircraft on their

SAS greatcoat buttons and a cuff button. (Private collection/Jenny Morgan)

Maj the Earl Jellicoe (left), SBS Commander, with Capt Chevilier on board Special Boat Squadron headquarters boat Tewfik, c. 1944. (IWM HU71413)

Did you know?

Which son of a British Prime Minister accompanied David Stirling and his SAS raiders on a mission in the Western Desert? Answer: Randolph Churchill, son of the legendary premier Winston.

lightning raids. Stirling was promoted to major in January 1942 and enlarged his unit with more recruits, including a Company of Free French paratroopers under the command of Capt Berge, which became the French Squadron of the SAS. Another crack unit to come under Stirling's wing was the Special Boat Section of No. 8 Commando. A combined SAS and Commando SBS raiding force was transported to Bouerat in January 1942 by the LRDG and despite the canoe which was to be used in the raid being damaged en route, the raiders' bombs devastated the harbour facilities. In March the same year, Stirling attacked Benghazi harbour. Again the boat was damaged, but the irrepressible Paddy Mayne destroyed around fifteen aircraft at Berka. The tough fighters of the Greek Sacred Squadron joined Stirling's flourishing SAS L Detachment. This squadron was made up of former officers and men of the Greek Army who had escaped the Nazi occupation of their homeland and were champing at the bit to wreak revenge on the Germans, which they did in bloodthirsty fashion.

The SAS received secret orders to stop the Luftwaffe sinking a vital convoy bound for Malta. Raiding parties hit airfields at

Cpl John Henderson Melville, L Detachment SAS, with heavy Browning jeep machine gun in the Western Desert, 1943. (IWM E21343)

Benghazi, Barce, Derna and Heraklion on Crete. The Crete raid, led by Berge and British and Free French SAS, damaged the airfield but was decimated. Earl Jellicoe,

later Commander of the Special Boat Service, escaped to safety with a Greek guide, but the rest of the party were killed or taken prisoner and shot, including Berge.

The raiding capabilities of the SAS were transformed with a consignment of jeeps from America. Stirling spotted their potential for desert raiding; they could be fitted with machine guns and would give the SAS independence from the LRDG. Like modern cars, their radiators had simple condensers, which enabled the jeeps to cope with the fierce desert temperatures. Water expanded into the condensers in the heat of the day and drained back into the radiators at night. As a result, the vehicles did not overheat so often. Stirling found some obsolete RAF Vickers K drum-fed machine guns which were bound for scrap. These guns had a very high rate of fire – more than 1,000 rounds a minute – and were designed to shoot up and set ablaze aircraft in air-to-air combat, their ammunition comprising a deadly mixture of tracer, armour-piercing and explosive bullets. Twin sets of the machine guns were mounted front and rear on the SAS jeeps which, with extra jerry cans strapped onto the rear and bonnet, had an extended range of several hundred

Billy Hull's brass SAS cap badge, presented to the author by his friend Gary, Billy's son. Billy was a courageous Second World War SAS soldier from Northern Ireland and member of 1st SAS Regiment who was Mentioned in Despatches for bravery and was Paddy Mayne's driver after D-Day. (Jenny Morgan)

The scene was set for one of the most famous SAS raids of the Second World War – The Big Jeep Raid. The target was Sidi Haneish, a landing ground in the Fuka area housing a large number of JU 52 transport planes, in short supply at this crucial stage of the Desert War. Stirling's plan used surprise and massive firepower from more than seventy machine guns on the jeeps to destroy as many planes as possible in one devastating raid in the light of the full moon. Eighteen jeeps drove at the base in line abreast, shooting up the perimeter defences. Then, blasting on to the airfield, a green Very light was fired and the jeeps

miles. The renowned transport of the SAS was in action. Browning .5in heavy machine guns were also mounted on some jeeps to give further firepower.

changed formation into an arrowhead, headed by Stirling's vehicle. The SAS raiders drove straight between the densely packed rows of planes. All their machine guns opened up simultaneously with devastating results, blasting the Nazi planes to pieces and setting them on fire. There were also Stukas and Messerschmitts on the airfield. Exploding petrol tanks ripped the night sky as plane after plane was blown up. The heat was so intense that some of the British men's eyebrows were singed and German troops were seen running about in panic, silhouetted by the flames.

Stirling's jeep was hit by a stray burst of fire and put out of action, but another jeep raced by to pick up him and his crew. A heavy enemy machine gun caused the only SAS casualty of the action, killing a front gunner. Return fire from the SAS jeeps silenced all opposition. Stirling then ordered his men to destroy some remaining planes on the edge of the airfield as the raiders prepared to roar away into the desert. The airfield was a scene of utter chaos, but the rest of the SAS got away without a scratch and hid camouflaged under scrub in the desert until the fuss died down. This one big raid, and a smaller one nearby, accounted for at least 50 enemy aircraft – a running total after a year's operations of around 250 destroyed. Afterwards, the Germans guarded each plane individually and though jeep raids were mounted on other occasions, they were never repeated on this huge scale. It was a magnificent one-off, so typical of Stirling's flamboyant daring.

In August 1942, the Special Boat Section of Middle East Commando came under SAS control. Earl Jellicoe and Fitzroy Maclean

Second World War 2nd SAS re-enactment group in maroon berets chat to comrades from the 1st SAS in the jeep who are wearing the famous beige berets, 'somewhere behind the lines in France'. (John Blackman)

Legendary .303 Bren light machine gun Mk 1 (top) and the later 7.32 light machine gun, both used in many campaigns by the SAS from the Second World War to the Oman and beyond. (John Blackman)

organised units under the SAS umbrella, which later emerged as the Special Boat Squadron. L Detachment was now renamed the 1st Special Air Service, a regiment in its own right with a strength of about 400. Stirling's command comprised: 1st SAS, 500 all ranks; French SAS Squadron, around 100 all ranks; Greek Sacred Squadron, 115 all ranks; Special Boat Section, 55 all ranks. A 2nd SAS Regiment was formed by

Stirling's brother William, who began training with the American 1st Army which had landed in Africa in the Operation Torch invasion in November 1942. As related earlier, disaster struck in January 1943 when Stirling was captured by a German counter-SAS unit in the Gabes area of Tunisia while attempting to link up with American forces for the first time. He made several bold escape attempts, but was eventually incarcerated in Colditz Castle until the war's end.

Paddy Mayne took over as Commander of the 1st SAS, which was split in two to prepare for raids in support of the Allied invasions of Sicily and Italy. He kept the SAS in existence, operating as the temporarily renamed Special Raiding Squadron, despite criticism from the doubters in the High Command. The other half of 1st SAS comprised 250 men under Earl Jellicoe as the Special Boat Squadron, based near Haifa. With the Greek Sacred Squadron, they raided enemy-occupied Mediterranean and Aegean islands and the Adriatic.

Never a stranger to controversy – or of having to fight for its existence against jealous high-ranking officers on its own side – the SAS prepared for its next battles, one of which, Termoli, in Italy, would be its toughest ever test.

A common misconception is that the SAS have fought in many battles as the elite infantry of the British Army. In reality nothing could be further from the truth. The SAS was the first true Special Force and the purpose of soldiers of the Regiment is to ghost into a key area of operation, do their clandestine jobs as unobtrusively as possible, unless involving a direct assault on an objective, and then ghost out again – preferably undetected by the enemy.

Sometimes SAS troopers take on the garb of local civilians of various countries and nationalities so they can operate freely within their chosen area. This was the case in some of the SAS operations in the Second World War, especially in the Western Desert, although in that conflict the Regiment did see an enormous amount of fighting, as the SAS was in continuous action from 1941 to 1945. This mostly took the form of small-scale raids on foot and in jeeps in the Western Desert and amphibious raiding operations in Sicily and Italy in 1943. Later, the SAS was behind the massive Para drops and raids in support of the Allied invasion of France in 1944 and in Belgium and Holland, in addition to motorised incursions into Holland and Germany supporting and scouting for the main armies in the final defeat of the Nazi empire. Some of these operations involved scores of men in heavily armed jeeps and caused huge casualties among the Germans, though none of these could ever be described as battles. Nevertheless, the destruction wreaked by the raiding parties of the SAS was out of proportion to the unit's size in all theatres of the war.

Did you know?

At times in the Second World War veterans say that SAS soldiers wore green Commando berets in action – presumably when the others were in short supply.

'Every one of my chaps was killed . . . the chap I was talking to through the truck's window was blown to pieces and I wasn't touched. It was quite mad.'

Capt Johnny Wiseman, 1st SAS, the sole survivor of his troop after a German shell scored a direct hit on their truck at the height of the battle of Termoli, Italy.

In the Western Desert the SAS destroyed more than 400 of Germany's best fighters and bombers, and in France and Germany after D-Day they killed thousands of enemy troops, destroyed hundreds of vehicles and many trains, countless ammunition and fuel dumps, and many other key targets.

There *was* one true infantry battle in which the SAS was involved, the battle of Termoli in Italy in 1943 during the Second World War. It was often described as a 'hell on earth' by the soldiers who fought and won the conflict. The British High Command was in a desperate, near critical, position at the time. Powerful German forces were threatening a breakthrough in the Termoli area which could have outflanked the main army which was advancing northwards through Italy.

Rare metal SAS officer's cap badge from the desert days, 1942. (Private collection/Jenny Morgan)

Replica Second World War SAS jeep showing jerry cans which carried petrol and drinking water, and camouflage netting used in bivouacs and to give quick concealment from searching enemy aircraft and ground troops. (John Blackman)

➤

Front row, left to right: Maj Sandy Scratchley and Roy Farran of 2nd SAS after the battle of Termoli, 1943. (IWM E26182)

The 1st SAS was operating temporarily as the Special Raiding Squadron (SRS) and this force, as well as elements of the 2nd SAS Regiment and key Commando units, was hastily gathered together and thrown into action via an amphibious landing to plug the gap. Fighting with great courage and tenacity – on this occasion as infantry soldiers – they withstood countless violent assaults by their opponents, who were fanatical, elite German parachute shock troops. The Germans attacked in great numbers, supported by tanks, mortars and artillery, while the SRS/SAS had light machine guns, mortars and whatever artillery and air support they could call in from the British and American forces. The British took heavy casualties, including twenty-nine SRS troops who were boarding a truck in the town ready to repulse an

Twin Vickers K machine guns on a replica SAS jeep. (Picture by John Blackman)

Did you know?
Despite being turned down for what many people believe was his rightful award of a VC, Lt Col Robert Blair 'Paddy' Mayne – the outstanding Commander of the SAS in the Second World War – became Britain's most highly decorated officer of the war.

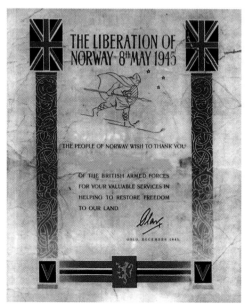

attack, when a shell or mortar scored a direct hit, killing nearly all of them. Despite these overwhelming odds, none of the SAS or Commandos involved would give an

Brace of replica Second World War SAS jeeps with various heavy armaments. (John Blackman)

inch over several days of heavy fighting, before reinforcements arrived.

SAS officer Johnny Wiseman, a veteran of 1st SAS, and many of the troops involved were convinced afterwards that the SRS/SAS could have been wiped out in this one-sided battle, but for the determination of the combined British Special Forces to win through.

At the time, October 1943, American forces had captured Naples, but well dug in and heavily defended German positions were frustrating their drive north. A bold and quick Allied response was urgently needed in the Termoli area and the SRS was sent into action via an amphibious landing with two other tough British units, Nos 3 and 40 Commando, to seize two key bridges and then hold on and wait for the main army to arrive via reinforcement by

sea. The assault group left Manfredonia on the Adriatic, south of Termoli, in an American LCI landing craft. The SRS swiftly advanced inland from its beachhead and over a railway line, then through No. 3 Commando's bridgehead and up the road towards Vasto, a coastal town a few miles north of Termoli. This move alarmed the Germans, who feared a tactical advance

By the KING'S Order the name of
Trooper W. Hull,
Army Air Corps
was published in the London Gazette on
29 March, 1945.
as mentioned in a Despatch for distinguished service.
I am charged to record
His Majesty's high appreciation.

Secretary of State for War

47

Veteran SAS Spr Sgt Roy 'Darkie' Chappell (Royal Engineers) HQ Squadron 1st SAS, 1945. Roy saw action in the Second World War in the desert; in Sicily – including destroying coastal defence gun batteries south of Syracuse in an amphibious raid led by Maj Paddy Mayne; in France after D-Day and in Germany as part of Operation Howard, to final victory in 1945. (Courtesy of Dave Mundy)

developing to the north of Rome, which could have helped to break the deadlock on the Italian mainland. They unleashed a violent counter-attack, the first of many, throwing into the battle the elite veterans of the 1st Parachute Division which was rapidly moved in from the Anzio area. This bloody battle had progressed from Allied amphibious, behind-the-lines masterstroke to disastrous stalemate and cost the lives of many thousands of Allied servicemen – all due to the inability of the American-led forces to exploit the key initial surprise of the landing. Meanwhile, the Germans moved into the Termoli battleground their 16th Panzer Division, which was being held in reserve near Naples.

The German orders, which later fell into British hands, were to recapture Termoli 'at all costs' and drive the British back into the sea. Had it not been for the tenacious courage and fighting skills of the SRS and 2nd SAS and their Commando comrades, they would have done just that.

Maj Roy Farran, the legendary 2nd SAS officer, who had seen action in the Western Desert and Crete in tanks, found the Termoli battle against the elite German troops and tanks one of the toughest of his career. A powerful German thrust seized the key cemetery area of the town, forcing the SRS/SAS back on to the last ridge before the railway goods yard. Farran said in his

'We doggedly stuck it out and beat off crack troops equipped with tanks and artillery – and took everything the Germans threw at us.'

L/Cpl Denis Bell, 1st SAS/SRS, on the battle of Termoli, Italy.

book *Winged Dagger*: 'Although we only had the strength of 20 men, our firepower was abnormally strong. In all, there were 6 Brens and a 2-inch mortar. I covered our 1,000-yard front between the 1st SAS and the sea by putting ten men with three Brens on each side of the railway line. Our main trouble was that we had no tools with which to dig weapon pits. In spite of the fact that heavy fire was directed on us from the cemetery and that constant attempts were made to advance down the line of the railway, we held our position for three days.'

At Termoli, Desert SAS veteran Reg Seekings DCM, MM, had to rush to report to Lt Col Paddy Mayne that another serious counter-attack was underway. The situation was critical and a breakthrough imminent, but as Seekings hurried into the monastery, which was being used as SRS headquarters, Mayne – the SRS Commander – was coolly playing snooker with some of his officers. Despite the fact that German shells were crashing down all around, Mayne insisted on completing his shot before mustering his forces up to the cemetery to meet and beat the German attack, which included tanks.

SAS veteran, the late L/Cpl Denis Bell, told the author that the battle of Termoli was one of the toughest actions in which the SRS and 2nd SAS were involved. He said: 'For a time, it was touch and go before we forced the numerically superior German units to withdraw.'

The horrors – and heroism – of Termoli will always be remembered in pride of place in the illustrious battle honours of the SAS.

Did you know?

SAS soldiers Bronco Lane and Brummie Stokes made a successful assault on the summit of Everest in 1986.

1st and 2nd SAS re-enactors meet up in a farmyard 'behind-the-lines somewhere in enemy territory during the Second World War'. (John Blackman)

No one will ever know precisely what tasks the SAS would have performed in the Cold War era from the 1960s to the early 1990s, because Russia and the countries of the Eastern Bloc, and their adversaries, the United States, Britain and the European NATO allies, did not start a shooting war during this long period of intense mistrust, blatant threats and, at times, outright hostility.

Most military experts believe the Cuban missile crisis of 1962 when, at the last possible minute, Russia turned back ships carrying a cargo of nuclear missiles to be sited on America's doorstep with the connivance of Cuban leader Fidel Castro, to be the nearest anyone has ever got to starting a Third World War. Roy Percival, an eyewitness who at the time was living near a missile base near Melton Mowbray, saw, along with many others, American nuclear intercontinental ballistic missiles up and out of their silos, firing up their motors and running all night long, as the world held its breath. He said: 'We could clearly hear the rocket motors and the noise was horrendous. We actually thought that some had been fired off at the time and that the World War had started. It was terrifying.' Both sides were literally waiting for the order to 'go' as the point of no return was almost reached. At that moment, the Russian leader Nikita Khrushchev ordered the convoy to turn and head for home and he and American president John Kennedy took their fingers off the destruct buttons. The same scenario was repeated at military bases around the world and, miraculously, peace was preserved.

The 'beads and ridges' Fairbairn Sykes SAS knife, 1941–3, made by Rogers of Sheffield and considered the finest and best balanced wartime dagger of all. (Private collection/Jenny Morgan)

Artists Rifles SAS officer's cartridge belt badge, 21 SAS, c. 1947. (Private collection/Jenny Morgan)

For most of the Cold War, Russia and the West maintained substantial conventional forces of troops, tanks, warplanes and artillery facing one another along the border of the Soviet Eastern Bloc. The Russians had overwhelming superiority in numbers of soldiers and tanks, although it has since been argued that the high quality of troops,

Armed SAS jeep of the type used by 2nd SAS in occupied Europe, 1944–5. (John Blackman)

Did you know?

SAS Tpr Tom McClean rowed single-handedly across the Atlantic in just seventy days in 1969. An outstanding feat.

tanks, equipment and airpower of the West could have offset the more numerous, but sometimes inferiorly equipped Soviet forces. If hostilities had commenced the SAS would have conducted similar operations to those it carried out behind German lines in the Second World War.

Infiltrators would have been inserted in small teams, perhaps by parachute, or by going to ground and emerging on sabotage missions. They would have let the advancing elements of the Red Army pass them by, before coming out of hiding to carry out pre-arranged and carefully planned covert missions behind enemy lines in small, flexible teams consisting of a handful of men. These tactics, like those of their 1st and 2nd SAS forefathers in the Second World War, would have involved secretive tasks such as reporting troop and armoured movements, calling down air strikes on key targets and carrying out numerous acts of sabotage and clinically planned mayhem. Each small squad would have worked independently of the others so that if captured, the other teams would not have been compromised by any comrades being interrogated under duress, or at least would have kept this to an absolute minimum. The only downside if hostilities

Wartime veteran's gold and silver bullion SAS blazer badge, made in Portsmouth by Chinese tailor Lee. (Private collection/Jenny Morgan)

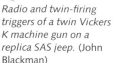

Radio and twin-firing triggers of a twin Vickers K machine gun on a replica SAS jeep. (John Blackman)

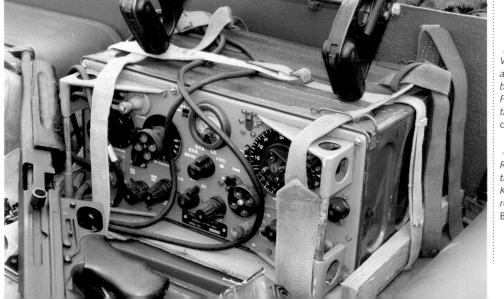

had commenced in this way was that SAS participants throughout this highly dangerous period would have been, as one veteran told me 'expendable'. As in the Second World War and most other conflicts the SAS has been involved in, once behind enemy lines each soldier or officer is entirely on their own and, if anything goes wrong, no help can be offered, or is expected. Any SAS not killed outright in action by the Soviets could have faced

'If the Cold War had broken out, it can be assumed that the role of the SAS would have been very similar to the one in which the Regiment was engaged during the Second World War, with units operating deep behind enemy lines.'

Retired SAS WOII Geordie Doran.

brutal interrogation as they did from the SS and Gestapo in the Second World War. Whether they would have been tortured and shot by the Russian Communists, as they were in harrowing circumstances when caught by the Nazis under Hitler's infamous Commando Order, will never be known. There are no guarantees in war, only surprises – and in the cold light of day many of these turn out to be unpleasant.

Suffice it to say that no matter how brave, or effective, the SAS Regiment would have been during the Cold War period, once either side had started to lose significantly, the temptation to use tactical, or full-scale, nuclear weapons en masse to restore the balance, or ultimately to stop an invasion of European or Russian territory, would have been overwhelming and – some experts say – inevitable.

SAS machine gunners in live firing training with US Browning medium machine guns, 1959. (Geordie Doran)

Thus, in this entirely hypothetical scenario, all the efforts, skill and courage of the SAS could have counted for nothing. It is a very sobering thought. However, it is certain that the soldiers of the SAS would have carried out their orders to the last and to the letter, no matter how uncertain the outcome – and victories have sometimes been snatched from the most unpromising of circumstances.

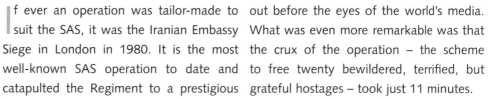

Browning .5 machine gun and bullet-proof protection for a gunner on a replica SAS jeep. (John Blackman)

If ever an operation was tailor-made to suit the SAS, it was the Iranian Embassy Siege in London in 1980. It is the most well-known SAS operation to date and catapulted the Regiment to a prestigious place at the top of the Special Forces scene, as the whole dramatic incident was played out before the eyes of the world's media. What was even more remarkable was that the crux of the operation – the scheme to free twenty bewildered, terrified, but grateful hostages – took just 11 minutes.

It is doubtful whether any other unit in the world could have achieved the same result at that time. The SAS had been training specifically for crises such as this for years and was well-prepared and confident in the ability of its soldiers, who were all hand-picked, experienced men. The many hours spent practising in the Killing House at the SAS Hereford base, shooting at targets which popped up randomly, mimicking the real-life situations which could occur in a mass hostage situation, paid off handsomely. Prime Minister Margaret Thatcher and a relieved and proud British public were incredibly impressed by the

fashion possible in the modern era of Special Operations and had proved it was not only here to stay, but was indisputably the best there is. It had already paved the way for that premier honour in the Second World War against the might of Nazi Germany and later against terrorism in the jungles of Malaya and Borneo and again in battle in the deserts of Oman and Yemen. The tough challenge now was to stay at the top by maintaining the high standards always expected of the world's finest.

The storming of the embassy at Prince's Gate in Kensington, codenamed Operation Nimrod, was to go down in history as a textbook success, the lessons of which would be pored over and emulated by rival Special Forces worldwide, although sadly not always resulting in the same minimum casualties among the hostages.

operation – not to mention numerous foreign nations, leading politicians and military figures worldwide. Put simply, the SAS had arrived in the most spectacular

A replica Second World War SAS jeep showing Vickers K drum-fed machine guns, Browning machine gun and the distinctive bullet-proof semi-circular glass shields and accompanying armour plate at the front of the vehicle. (John Blackman)

The drama flared up when six terrorists, known as the Democratic Revolutionary Movement for the Liberation of Arabistan, seized the embassy at 11.30 a.m. on 30 April 1980, grabbing twenty-six terrified hostages. The terrorists wanted autonomy for Khuzestan, an oil-rich region in southern Iran, and demanded the release of ninety-one of their comrades from Iranian jails. Five hostages were freed over the first few days after specially trained police negotiators opened talks with the terrorists. The situation worsened on the third day when the terrorists threatened to kill a hostage. They were trying to force

'This mission really put the SAS in the world spotlight.'

Retired SAS WOII Geordie Doran on the Iranian Embassy Siege.

◄

Modern-day SAS fatigue wings and officer's wire wing badges. (Private collection/Jenny Morgan)

the Jordanian ambassador to provide safe passage for their group. On the sixth day of the siege the terrorists killed press attaché hostage Abbas Lavasani and threw his body outside. Prime Minister Thatcher gave the go-ahead to the Counter Revolutionary Warfare wing of the SAS to mount a rescue operation. The Metropolitan Police handed over control to the military and plans to assault the embassy and free as many hostages as possible went ahead.

Several cunning diversions were used before the 'Who Dares Wins' heroes put their lives on the line and stormed into action. The government sanctioned lower landing paths for planes coming into Heathrow Airport and Gas Board workmen began an almighty racket digging up a nearby street with pneumatic drills to mask the approach of the SAS squads. High-

tech microphones and fibre-optic probes were bored into the wall of the embassy from the next door building to track the movements of the terrorists and gauge where the hostages were being held at gunpoint. The date of the assault, Bank Holiday Monday 5 May 1980, was about

Replica SAS jeep of the type used in occupied Europe during 1944–5. Note the heavy machine gun mounted in the rear. (John Blackman)

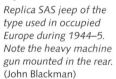
Rare SAS dress wings from the 1950s. (Private collection/Jenny Morgan)

to go down in history with a bang – several big ones in fact! Electrical power was cut to the building and, simultaneously, the SAS went in just after 7.20 p.m., within minutes of the first hostage being murdered.

The SAS, dressed in black, with hoods, goggles and respirators and carrying MP 5 sub-machine guns, climbed into the building via an adjoining balcony at the front, lobbing stun grenades inside with a terrific noise and flash. Others abseiled down from the roof at the rear and blasted in upper windows and frames with special explosives. The spectacular entry via the balcony at the front was captured by TV cameras trained on the building for audiences worldwide to see live. An explosive charge was also detonated in a

'Probably the greatest siege-busting operation ever.'

SAS and Royal Marines veteran Tommo Thomson, who knew most of the SAS men involved in the Iranian Embassy Siege.

stairwell and more SAS soldiers raced inside in the deliberate confusion. Stun grenades were liberally thrown to disorientate the terrorists during the lightning attack. Five of the six terrorists were shot dead and nineteen hostages saved unharmed, but one was killed by a terrorist during the attack.

The BBC interrupted coverage of the World Snooker Championships and correspondent Kate Adie reported the drama live for 45 minutes, to a massive audience nationwide, while crouching

◄

Geordie Doran of the SAS in the Malayan jungle in the early 1960s holding a self-loading semi-automatic rifle. (Geordie Doran)

behind a car. Later there was controversy over the killing of some of the gunmen, as hostages had persuaded them to throw down their guns and surrender. However, a subsequent coroner's inquest absolved the SAS soldiers of blame, as they believed the terrorists were going for their weapons, or for hidden grenades. The surviving gunman was found cowering among the hostages and was arrested. Fowzi Nejad was sentenced to life in prison for his part in the siege.

A jubilant Margaret Thatcher and husband Denis visited the SAS at their Regent's Park barracks after the siege personally to thank those who took part in and planned the operation. More than thirty SAS troopers had stormed the embassy – and carved an indelible niche for themselves in history. The hostages were mostly Iranians, plus embassy police guard PC Trevor Lock, some BBC staff and tourists collecting visas.

Some sources claimed the terrorists were sponsored by the then Iraqi president Saddam Hussein. It was said that Iraq had trained and armed the gunmen in order to embarrass Iran – at that time its number one enemy. The siege later helped to fuel a war between Iran and Iraq, which cost many hundreds of thousands of lives on both sides.

The SAS Regiment played a prominent role in both Gulf Wars. However, a great deal more is known about its contribution to the First Gulf War than to the Second and the explanation for this lack of information can be summed up in three famous, some would say infamous, words: Bravo Two Zero!

As will be recounted in more detail below, Sgt Andy McNab (pseudonym) and the SAS men under his command on this code-named operation, became known after the First Gulf War in 1991 for their patrol behind Iraqi lines, which was the subject of a best-selling book (*The One That Got Away*) and follow-up account by the one SAS man who evaded capture and made it back to Allied lines, Chris Ryan MM. For various reasons, including a duff radio, appalling weather and sheer bad luck, the men of Bravo Two Zero made early contact with the enemy. Some died, others were captured and their mission became an unmitigated disaster – despite the courage and sacrifice of those involved.

Ironically, other SAS teams who *were* successful in their missions – including those searching for and destroying Scud missiles which were being fired towards Israel by Saddam Hussein in an attempt to widen the conflict – did not receive the same amount of recognition and publicity in the media and elsewhere. Similarly, those involved in fighting column incursions deep into the Iraqi desert, using vehicles bristling with machine guns reminiscent of the fighting jeeps and trucks of their Second World War forefathers, were also eclipsed by the huge amount of interest generated in the McNab mission.

Brass SAS cap badge made by REME soldiers for the SAS in Italy during 1943. (Private collection/ Katie Morgan)

An SAS re-enactor displays the distinctive beige beret, 'Who Dares Wins' badge of the Regiment, and camouflaged smock, while sighting a British SLR rifle, the mainstay of the British Army until replaced by the current SA80 weapon in the 1990s. (John Blackman)

After the war, SAS and Ministry of Defence chiefs judged that too much information had been aired in public in various books and the media, and all serving SAS personnel were required to sign disclosure agreements which effectively banned them from disclosing or writing about conflicts in which they had been involved. Hence virtually all the information about the activities of the SAS found in the national press or on television came from journalists' own sources and contacts. The SAS and the powers that be reasoned that lives could be put at risk by unchecked disclosures and that secret missions, or descriptions of methods of SAS operation, could be compromised and information leaked to an enemy. These 'leaks' were plugged, with the result that the public has been kept in the dark about

SAS veteran's cap badges from the Malaya campaign. (Private collection/Jenny Morgan)

the activities of their favourite Special Forces regiment.

As the First Gulf War, code-named Desert Storm, was about to get underway, the Commander-in-Chief of the Allied forces was Gen Norman Schwarzkopf, a tough but well-liked Vietnam veteran. Initially he was a lukewarm supporter of Special Forces of any kind, but by the end of the war, the successes of the SAS in particular had made him a firm convert. Significantly,

Pink Panthers aren't big cats – they are special four-wheel drive vehicles heavily armed with general purpose 0.5 machine guns and a host of other weapons. They were used by the SAS in the desert in the First Gulf War against Iraq. It was noted in the Second World War that pink is one of the best colours for camouflage in the desert.

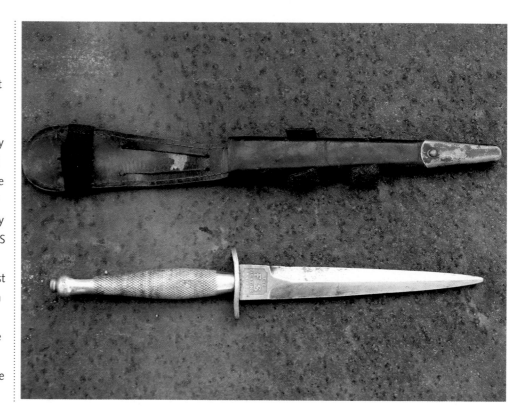

'The roving motorised patrols in the desert in Iraq looked uncannily like those commanded by David Stirling in the Second World War fifty years before.'

Retired SAS WOII Geordie Doran.

Lt Gen Peter de la Billiere, Commander of the British Forces, was a veteran former Commander of 22 SAS and his influence was undoubtedly a key factor in this change of heart. The SAS Regiment deployed to the Gulf just after Christmas 1990, with A, B and D Squadrons flying out. An early plan for the SAS and US Delta Force to rescue foreign 'human shield' hostages, held under the orders of Iraqi president Saddam Hussein, often near or at key Allied targets, was ditched as unworkable.

By mid-January 1991, the SAS was operating in advance of the main attack, knocking out Iraqi communications and searching for the infamous Scud missile launchers. These were often very difficult to see from the air and required eyes on the ground to locate and destroy them. When a massive air attack was unleashed on Iraq in January, marking the official start of the war, Saddam Hussein ordered his Scuds to strike back, trying to provoke Israel into retaliation and cause a widening of the war among other Arab nations. Some of the SAS squads were sent deep into enemy territory by helicopter and their teams were given a priority mission to find and destroy the mobile Scud launchers. Others marked targets with laser designators and these were soon blasted by Allied aircraft. In a move reminiscent of their founding fathers of the Long Range Desert Group in the Second World War, other squads mounted

Did you know?
Gen Sir Peter de la Billiere, Commander of the British Forces during the First Gulf War, was a highly experienced and decorated SAS officer, holder of the Distinguished Service Order and Military Cross.

Fairbairn Sykes fighting knife and scabbard as used by the SAS. This is an early Wilkinson Sword model identifiable by the distinctive wavy hilt. (John Blackman)

road watch patrols to report on enemy vehicle and convoy targets to be attacked from the air. Heavily armed, mobile desert fighting columns also probed the enemy's fighting resolve and carried out search and destroy missions, usually at night. They would rest during the day, camouflaged with netting and desert scrub, away from any prying Iraqi eyes.

The fighting columns were made up of up to twelve type 110 Land Rovers – sometimes with motorcycle outriders, although these proved vulnerable to enemy fire. Armament of the main vehicles included a Browning .50 cal. heavy machine gun, general purpose machine guns, Milan anti-tank missiles of the type used currently in Iraq and Afghanistan and American 40mm grenade launchers. The SAS columns operated deep inside Iraq at will during the entire war.

◄ ◄
Geordie Doran of the SAS after exiting a de Havilland Rapide at Chalon-sur-Saône, training Para airfield in France, 1961. (Geordie Doran)

◄
SAS Gulf War sergeant veteran's insignia of 22 SAS, c. 1991. This experienced soldier also completed three tours of duty in Northern Ireland. (Private collection/Jenny Morgan)

Did you know?
The 'one that got away' who took part in the Bravo Two Zero SAS mission in the First Gulf War was Chris Ryan. He won a well-deserved Military Medal for getting back to British lines single-handed, through many miles of enemy territory.

The weather was unusually cold and some of the men contracted hypothermia and frostbite but, in a tribute to the skill and training of the SAS, only four soldiers were lost in the conflict. By the end of the war, around a third of the Scud launchers had been knocked out by the SAS and the Regiment had won fifty-five medals for gallantry. The previously doubting Allied Commander, Gen Schwarzkopf, now praised the SAS to the hilt.

BRAVO TWO ZERO SAGA

Eight SAS members of the Bravo Two Zero SAS squad were helicoptered into Iraq on the night of 22 January 1991. In addition to locating and destroying mobile Scud missiles, their task was to mount a covert watch on the main enemy supply route and tip-off HQ about any developments. The cutting of underground communications cables between Baghdad and Jordan, causing the enemy forces even more chaos, was another target. However, several parts of the mission soon went badly wrong. Crucially, their radio was not working. The patrol was virtually helpless without communications, operating so deep in Iraqi territory. Events rapidly worsened when the patrol made contact with the enemy, eventually resulting in a fire fight. After giving an excellent account of themselves and causing many casualties among the Iraqi soldiers opposing them, the SAS patrol retreated and tried to escape into the desert, making for the Syrian border about 120km away. But the terrible weather resulted in patrol members separating – some were badly affected by hypothermia. Just one man, Chris Ryan, succeeded in getting

safely to the Syrian border. All the SAS men showed great courage and determination, but three died as a result of the cold, or their injuries, and four – including Patrol Leader Sgt Andy McNab – were captured and tortured by the Iraqis. At the end of the war they were released and, when they had recovered, returned to the Regiment to tell their dramatic tale.

After liberating Kuwait and advancing deep into Iraqi territory, the Allied armies halted their advance short of Baghdad. They did not take the city and overthrow the dictator Saddam Hussein, as many experts urged them to do. It was a decision the American and British Armies were later to regret.

* * *

The Second Gulf War broke out on 20 March 2003. The American, British and

Vickers K machine gun and jeep mounting. (John Blackman)

75

Allied objective this time was to topple Saddam Hussein by annihilating his military and civilian power base. This was achieved by a missile and bombing campaign and major ground attack. It has since become clear that the SAS and various other Special Forces from the Coalition, including the Australian SAS, US Delta Force and Navy SEALS, had slipped across the border into Iraq well in advance of the air war. Their mission, in part, as in the previous Gulf War, was to laser mark key targets for the strike aircraft to destroy by bombing.

Many more secret missions were carried out by the SAS during this Second Gulf War and much bravery was shown by members of the Special Air Service. However, the public will have to wait patiently for several years before the full details of the fascinating story of the SAS role in this crucial conflict is released.

'Overall in the Gulf, the SAS performed with great skill, bravery and professionalism.'

Retired SAS WOII Geordie Doran.

Geordie Doran and crew ranging a 3in mortar on to enemy targets during the assault on the Jebel el Akhdar, Oman, 1959. (Geordie Doran)

The SAS has actively operated in Iraq and Afghanistan for some years, but it would be foolish to pretend to know the extent of its activities other than to say that SAS soldiers have been called upon to utilise their considerable powers in infiltration, covert observation and taking the fight to the enemy where and when it is least expected.

One incident perhaps illustrates the crucial involvement of the SAS in these dangerous theatres of war more than any other. In

➤

Classic SAS-style sniper pose, as adopted in the Gulf War and other such desert landscapes where cunning and low-level concealment are key assets for survival. (John Blackman)

March 2002, there were announcements in regional and national newspapers and on the television that an SAS hero was to be awarded the VC after ferocious fighting in the Tora Bora cave complex in the White Mountains of Afghanistan. It was rumoured that Osama Bin Laden himself, the al-Qaeda leader, had been in the area when the SAS attacked and had narrowly escaped.

The Regimental Sergeant Major of the SAS at the time had, it was reported, shown particular bravery in desperate hand-to-hand fighting in the caves complex, as part of a 90-strong British force which was outnumbered at least two to one by terrorist forces. Leading from the front,

he had fought on despite being shot in the leg and had engaged in hair-raising close-quarter combat, which was said to include knives. The battle lasted 4 hours and the SAS emerged victorious, taking

'The fighting in the Tora Bora caves was heroism in the finest tradition of the SAS.'

Retired SAS WOII Geordie Doran.

◄
A group of SAS shoulder titles and a rarer 21 SAS shoulder title. (Private collection/Jenny Morgan)

➤

D Squadron SAS training on mortars at Ibri, Oman, 1961. (Geordie Doran)

➤➤

Top to bottom: Argentinian FN, British SLR and British L42 sniper rifle. The SAS came up against the Argentinian weapon during the Falklands War in which the Regiment played a prominent role. It also used SLRs in various actions and locations together with the sniper rifle, with scope for longer range targets. (John Blackman)

The phrase 'beating the clock' is used by SAS men who survive dangerous missions at home and abroad. The names of all SAS soldiers killed in action since the Second World War are inscribed on the clock tower at the SAS base at Credenhill, near Hereford. Hence those that survive unscathed are said to have 'beaten the clock'.

Maj Anders Lassen VC just before the Battle of Comacchio in which he was killed. (IWM HU71361)

D Squadron SAS members training on the then new 81mm mortar near Brecon, South Wales, in the mid-1960s. (Geordie Doran)

'Once again in Afghanistan, the SAS showed its courage and adaptability.'

Retired SAS WOII Geordie Doran.

Geordie Doran holding a Swedish Carl Gustav 9mm sub-machine gun, watching over a camel supply train during the Yemen secret mission, June/July 1963. (Geordie Doran)

the entire complex. The action was dubbed the Battle of the Caves and the unnamed RSM was reported to be earmarked to receive the Victoria Cross (VC) and become the first British SAS soldier ever to win the highest honour for gallantry. Maj Anders Lassen had won a supremely courageous VC at the end of the Second World War at Lake Comacchio, but he was a member of the sister unit of the SAS, the Special Boat Squadron, and was also a Danish recipient.

Geoff Hoon, the Defence Secretary at the time, was believed to have wanted the SAS soldier's identity to be revealed to bolster the prestige of the British presence in Afghanistan. Not surprisingly, given the sensitive nature of the secret work of the SAS, this did not happen and the identities of all the SAS soldiers involved were not made public.

A VC was not awarded to the RSM for reasons which have never fully become apparent. Instead, the two SAS members honoured for the action were awarded Conspicuous Gallantry Crosses – some of the highest awards for gallantry in the British Army. Thus the Special Air Service still awaits its first British recipient of the coveted VC.

The SAS has constantly changed and upgraded its tactics and methods of fighting and operation throughout its history, and the present day is no exception. It is not possible, or appropriate, to attempt to reveal its current methods in detail for reasons of security. Many of these well-practised methods are jealously guarded secrets upon which lives can depend. One of the reasons the SAS has been able to

Did you know?
In the storming of the Jebel Akhdar mountain stronghold in Oman in 1958, an attacking force of about 60 SAS officers and men scaled the mountain, took the rebels by surprise and defeated the enemy force of more than 600.

Modern machine gun weaponry of a replica SAS Pink Panther. (John Blackman)

stay ahead of the field for so long is that it is invariably the first Special Force to try something new. The Regiment, by its make up and modus operandi, is also exceedingly good at tight security and self-policing and in the ongoing battle against terrorism it keeps its cards close to its chest.

In some respects little has changed since the early days of the Regiment's foundation – the importance of stealth, covert observation, use of small-scale teams and behind-the-lines penetration are still relevant. In other respects, including the use of modern technology and weapons and the specialisation needed to combat threats such as hostage-taking and urban deployment, today's SAS soldier faces entirely new tasks.

The author can reveal some true stories about the SAS which richly illustrate not only the high level of skills which they achieve, but also how unorthodox methods are often encouraged as a key component in the armoury of every serving SAS man and officer.

Arthur Arger, of Middlesbrough, was an original member of Y Patrol of the Long Range Desert Group – forefathers of the SAS – and picked up David Stirling and what remained of his raiding force on their first disastrous mission in the Western Desert in 1941. Arthur was later captured on the Dodecanese islands and spent time in German prisoner-of-war camps before staging a daring escape. When he arrived back in Britain in 1945, after a period of convalescence, he was sent to an Army camp 'somewhere in Yorkshire' to await his demobilisation along with other soldiers, including a battle-hardened ex-member

The Mars and Minerva cap badge of 21 SAS. (Private collection/Jenny Morgan)

attention, he slowly lifted his arm to sight and fire the weapon once, twice and three times, but missed the glass bottles which had been lined as targets on a bank a few yards away.

Red-faced, he reloaded the weapon and turned to the man nearest to him, the rather scruffy, outwardly unimposing ex-SAS soldier. 'Here, see what you can do,' he barked, thrusting the pistol into the soldier's hand. The SAS man nonchalantly shrugged his shoulders and then suddenly dropped into the ultra-relaxed, instinctive, almost cowboy style of shooting which he had been taught in battle, rattling off six

of the SAS. One of the young officers in charge of the camp, who was wet behind the ears and had never seen any action, unwisely decided to try to teach these crack veterans, who had spent five years fighting a bitter World War, how to shoot a pistol. Demonstrating this skill to the motley gathering, standing stiffly to

'The SAS puts a strong emphasis on the need for superior close fighting skills.'

Retired SAS WOII Geordie Doran.

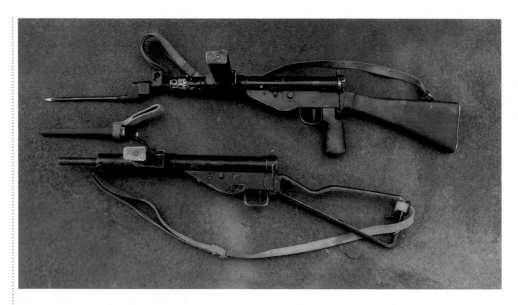

shots in rapid succession and blowing five out of the six bottles to oblivion. 'Must have been a lucky chance, I suppose,' he sniffed, handing the empty gun back to the stunned officer. Needless to say the shooting lesson was brought to an abrupt halt and was never repeated.

The SAS, from its earliest days, was taught that a 'double tap' method of shooting was usually the most effective

in action at close quarters. Instead of firing once at close range, it was found to be more deadly to fire twice in rapid succession. Also, in simple terms, it is often the case that if soldiers point their gun where they are looking and fire instinctively

An older SAS bullion officer's cap badge. This one has seen some action! (Private collection/Jenny Morgan)

Rear of a replica SAS jeep as used after D-Day, packed full of vital gear. (John Blackman)

they will hit the target more frequently than if they take careful aim in classic Bisley fashion. This method of firing, honed in the Second World War, takes practice to master and there are many exceptions these days where careful aim and different training do apply, such as hostage situations. But the SAS 'Killing House' exists in many respects to hone the sharp shooting skills of SAS soldiers.

Another SAS soldier explained how, in wartime situations, troopers were taught instinctively to draw and fire their pistols if they were unexpectedly attacked and fell to the ground. Surprisingly, it is possible to draw a pistol in mid-roll while falling and to aim, fire and despatch an enemy all in one smooth action (if you are a crack SAS soldier, that is).

Silent killing of an enemy sentry with a knife, using the classic Fairbairn Sykes Commando knife or modern equivalent, is not a pleasant prospect for any soldier but it is a task with which members of the Regiment have to be familiar with.

'Sometimes it's just you and the other man – and your bare hands.'

Retired SAS WOII Geordie Doran.

Here is a true tale courtesy of Gary Hull, from Belfast, whose father Billy was a 1st SAS veteran in the Second World War. It illustrates the point perfectly, with a touch of wicked black humour thrown in. An officer and Billy, of Barrington Street, Belfast – both comrades of the legendary 1st SAS Commander, Lt Col Paddy Mayne – approached a rail tunnel behind enemy lines on the outskirts of Paris in which they wanted to sabotage a train. There were two German sentries guarding the tunnel and the SAS raiders could not shoot the nearest, as that would have raised the alarm and alerted the other sentry, so there was only one outcome. To paraphrase their

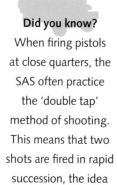

Did you know?

When firing pistols at close quarters, the SAS often practice the 'double tap' method of shooting. This means that two shots are fired in rapid succession, the idea being that if the first doesn't find its target, the second surely will.

conversation: 'We'll have to knife him,' said the officer. 'What say we toss a coin for it – and you can have first call?'

'Thanks sir,' whispered the SAS trooper. 'That's decent of you. I'll have heads.'

The coin was tossed into the air – heads it was!

'You're doing it anyway, we were tossing to decide the best job!' was the officer's terse reply and, with a shrug, the SAS soldier drew his razor sharp Commando knife and crept away to obey his superior's gruesome order to the letter.

Portrait of SAS Ulsterman Billy Hull. (Hull collection)

Friendly and professional links are fostered by the SAS with various Special Forces throughout the world, including the American Delta Force and the Australian and New Zealand Special Air Service

'Solid links with other Special Forces overseas are firm bonds for the good.'

Retired SAS WOII Geordie Doran.

➤
Replica SAS Pink Panther Land Rover, showing its equipment, spare wheels and an assortment of heavy weaponry. (John Blackman)

◄ A collection of vintage and modern pistols, similar examples of which have often been used in action by the SAS, including, from left, top to bottom: Walther, .38 Enfield, Browning Hi Power; right: Glock, Colt 45 and Luger. (John Blackman)

▲ Postwar officer's metal cap badge and collar dogs. (Private collection/ Jenny Morgan)

'The SAS has inspired the entire world in the formation of Special Forces.'

Retired SAS WOII Geordie Doran.

actively participated in the formation and training of some forces which are now well-established in their own right. Joint training exercises have been held, principally with the American units.

Other similar Special Forces, most of which have diligently taken on board the SAS ethos to a greater or lesser extent, include those from Belgium, Canada, France, Germany, Norway, Greece, Israel, Italy, Poland, Japan, Malaysia and the Netherlands.

Despite all the flattering imitation, most military experts agree that the original SAS is still the best there is.

Who dares contradict that?

The semi-circular bullet-proof glass protection and armour plate protecting the Vickers K gunner of an SAS jeep is clearly shown in this re-enactment study. (John Blackman)

Regiments, which are closely modelled on the original British SAS.

The Regiment has traditionally been regarded as an inspirational role model to most Special Forces worldwide and has

The SAS has always been at the forefront of the latest weapons and communications technology, experimentation in the means of insertion into enemy territory, survival techniques and training for every conceivable scenario for which it might be employed, and there is no reason to doubt whether this aspect of the pioneering Special Air Service will change in future.

The SAS has been the 'blueprint' for every other Special Force in the world and all eyes will remain on it in the future to see how it develops.

In twenty-five or even fifty years from now, though the equipment and tactics of the Regular British Army might be modernised and transformed beyond recognition, the role of Special Forces such as the SAS may alter to a lesser extent.

The threats and problems faced will vary markedly according to world politics. This has been especially true since the Second World War, through the very different conflicts in Malaya, Oman, the Falklands,

'There are no boundaries as to what the SAS can achieve in future.'

Retired SAS WOII Geordie Doran.

Modern 22 SAS wings. (Private collection/Jenny Morgan)

SAS members in Malaya just prior to operations in Oman, 1958. (Geordie Doran)

Did you know?
SAS soldiers call their officers Ruperts. This is a friendly term which began when several officers called Rupert joined the Regiment in the early days after the Second World War.

A contemporary example of an SAS officer's cloth cap badge. (Private collection/Jenny Morgan)

who can operate undetected behind enemy lines, either in a covert reconnaissance role to carry out sabotage or to guide warplanes, lasers or missiles on to targets. It is also probable that hostages will still be taken by various, as yet unknown, factions and that these pawns of ruthless ambition will still require an expert force which can rescue them as effectively as in the past.

Technology is evolving at a phenomenal pace and it is possible to speculate how the Regiment might take advantage of these developments in weapons, parachutes and life-protecting uniforms in future. It must be stressed that these are the author's ideas, arrived at through constructive interpretation of information which has been featured in the national media and not via any official, or unofficial comment or information obtained from any serving or

two Gulf Wars, Afghanistan, Iraq and other hot spots.

The fact is that even in fifty years' time it is likely that there will still be a place for small numbers of highly trained soldiers

retired member of the SAS, or other armed force. Some of the latest inventions and theories appear very way out at present, but many are already under development and in the early stages of being proven for the battlefield.

Rocket-powered batwing parachute
A civilian invention in its early stage of

development, this device is said to be capable, ultimately, of carrying a parachutist miles from the point of being dropped from an aeroplane, using an on-board rocket motor and built-in wings. Could we see a military form of this device

Colt AR15 M2 plus IWS – an advanced weapon as used by the SAS and other Special Forces. (John Blackman)

dropping Special Forces soldiers or secret agents 200 miles or more from a target in the future?

Uniforms that transform instantly to bullet-proof Special fabric is being investigated which can change from soft and pliable to rigid life-protecting material when struck by a bullet. This is not yet a reality, but, if as research suggests, it may be possible, and if such uniforms ever become available, the SAS could be one of the prime candidates to try them out in action.

Invisible cloaking Experiments have been carried out via light refraction incorporated in uniforms which could make soldiers either 'invisible' or very hard to detect by the naked eye. Apparently this technique could work in practice, but there is still a way to go.

The author has deliberately kept the descriptions of the above ideas non-scientific and highly simplified. However, even to the layman it can be seen that each could have an application for use by the SAS and probably other special British forces too. If these inventions are the cream of the publicised inventions and ideas, one wonders what is being developed on the secret list.

Getting back to reality, over the next decades the SAS will receive the best the world can offer in terms of hand and automatic guns and other weapons, explosives and equipment. All the weapons used by armed forces are constantly being refined and in future it is also likely that ammunition will be improved, making it lighter and more compact. The bullet itself may become redundant eventually if hand-held lasers, as seen in the comic books, ever become a reality. Whatever the invention, the SAS will – as it has always done – take it in its stride, test it thoroughly in all conditions, accept it if it does the job, but reject it if it doesn't.

In summary, of all the armed forces, the SAS is likely to be least changed by the passage of time. Its training, Selection, tactics and operations will probably be more similar to the present in years to come than many other units, with the courage, preparation, ingenuity and intelligence of its members ultimately more important than its resources.

Stirling's famous four-man teams of raiders will be operating deep behind enemy lines for many decades to come.

This is a chronological summary of the SAS Regiment's highlights from its creation in the Second World War to the present day. Many operations have been omitted to concentrate on the main points of history.

1941 Birth of the SAS The SAS is created in the Western Desert by David Stirling and named L Detachment, Special Air Service Brigade, to fool the Germans as to its size and strength. It later becomes 1st SAS Regiment and, for a short time, while

LRDG truck identical to those which picked up Stirling and his SAS raiders after their first disastrous mission in the Western Desert in 1941. (John Blackman)

Jimmy Laybourn (left), and Dave Morrison, 2nd SAS, with a captured Nazi flag on their jeep, Germany, 1945. (Courtesy of Steve James)

operating in Sicily and Italy, is renamed the Special Raiding Squadron (SRS), before reverting to 1st SAS for the rest of the war.

1943 The 2nd SAS Regiment is formed in Algeria, with Stirling's brother, William, as Commander.

1945 Disbandment In a shock move, the entire wartime SAS, 1st and 2nd British Regiments, 3rd and 4th French and 5th Belgian Regiments are all disbanded, or released from British control.

1947 21 Territorial SAS formed.

1950 Malaya Volunteers form the Malayan Scouts (SAS) to fight Communist guerrillas in jungle conditions in the Malayan Emergency.

SAS Capt Greville-Bell (third from left) talking with American troops in France, 1944. (Daniels collection)

1952 22 SAS Regiment is formed as the SAS expands and strengthens operations in Malaya. This unit soon becomes the backbone of the modern SAS. SAS squadrons remain in action in Malaya until early 1959.

1958–9 Oman 22 SAS deploys to the Gulf state of Oman and wins a brilliant campaign against forces trying to topple the Sultan.

1959 Territorial 23 SAS Regiment is formed.

1963–6 22 SAS fights Indonesian terrorists in Borneo, Brunei and Sarawak.

1970 Start of Dhofar conflict SAS returns to Oman as trouble flares once more.

1976 Northern Ireland troubles SAS is deployed to combat the growing threat of the IRA.

1980 Operation Nimrod Hand-picked members of various SAS squadrons storm the Iranian Embassy in London.

1982 Falklands War SAS plays a major role in assisting the main British forces in the liberation of the Islands after the Argentinian invasion.

1988 Gibraltar SAS shoots dead three IRA terrorists it believes are about to trigger a car bomb. An inquest into the deaths returns a verdict of lawful killing.

1991 First Gulf War SAS is sent to the Gulf after Saddam Hussein's invasion of Kuwait.

1995 Bosnia SAS supports UN peace-keepers.

1999 Kosovo SAS joins NATO action, including laser-guiding air strikes against the Serbs.

2000 Sierra Leone, Operation Barras SAS is at the forefront of a daring mission to free British soldiers seized by rebels.

2001 Afghanistan SAS is deployed in the wake of the terrorist attacks on 11 September in New York, USA.

2003 Second Gulf War, Iraq and the story to date SAS is deployed in a variety of roles, including hunting down top members of Saddam Hussein's regime and, in 2006, the rescue of British peace activist Norman Kember and two Canadian hostages from kidnappers in Baghdad.

2005 In the wake of the terrorist bombings in London in July, SAS and other UK Special Forces are deployed in mainland cities in a rapid-response role, supporting police.

2007 Afghanistan and Iraq – the war continues SAS squad snatches Taliban leader in troubled Helmand province of Afghanistan.